Dwayne's Guitar Lessons Present:

Lead Guitar Wizardry

Volume 1

By

Dwayne Jenkins

Copyright © 2019 Dwayne Jenkins
All Rights Reserved.
Published by Tritone Publishing

This book of spells and incantations will provide an essential guide on your journey to becoming a great lead guitarist. It will show you the secret formulas, scale patterns & techniques used by lead guitar wizards to create jaw-dropping guitar solos that capture the listener with magic.

Combine the study of this training manual with a regular daily practice routine, you will begin to develop skills you once thought were beyond your ability. Before you know it, you will be casting your own brand of guitar magic that will leave those listening in amazement.

But in order to do so you must study & practice on a daily basis. I can't stress the importance of this. It is vital to your development. Without it your progress will be slow & unfocused in which you might quit all together.

In doing so, you won't be able to reach your dream of being a lead guitar wizard.

So make a commitment to yourself, set your goals & develop a solid practice routine.

These two things alone will set a solid foundation for your success. And that is what most self taught students never develop, and in doing so they never get that far with their playing because they run into roadblocks that could of been avoided had they set up a solid foundation from the start.

So if you're ready,......Let's get started.

Table Of Contents

Module 1 Lead Guitar Basics 1
Lesson 1:   Introduction to notation   1
Lesson 2:   The 12 bar progression   5
Lesson 3:   Your major & minor scales   9
Lesson 4:   Guitar riffs to play over rhythm   11
Lesson 5:   Alternate picking & octaves   13

Module 2 Scales & Personality Licks 17
Lesson 6:   Pentatonic scale pattern 1   17
Lesson 7:   Triplets & transposing keys   19
Lesson 8:   Hammer ons & pull offs   21
Lesson 9:   Bends, slides & vibrato   23
Lesson 10: Combining techniques   26

Module 3   Key Progressions & Blues Scale 29
Lesson 11: Pattern 1 extended notes   29
Lesson 12: Major key progressions   31
Lesson 13: Minor key progressions   33
Lesson 14: Tremolo picking & trills   36
Lesson 15: Blues scale   38

Module 4   Additional Pentatonic Scale patterns 39
Lesson 16: Pentatonic scale pattern 2   39
Lesson 17: Pentatonic scale pattern 3   39
Lesson 18: Pentatonic scale pattern 4   39
Lesson 19: Pentatonic scale pattern 5   40
Lesson 20: Summary of all 5 scale patterns   41

Module 5   Scales With Additional Notes 43
Lesson 21:   Blues scale with additional notes   43
Lesson 22:   Major pentatonic scale with additional notes   43
Lesson 23:   Minor pentatonic scale with additional notes   44
Lesson 24:   Finger dexterity development   45
Lesson 25:   Tapping & repeated licks   47

Module 6   Harmony notes, Octaves & Hybrid Picking   49
Lesson 26:   Harmony notes in 3rd's   49
Lesson 27:   Harmony notes in 6th's   50
Lesson 28:   Creating with octaves   51
Lesson 29:   Hybrid picking   52
Lesson 30:   Sweep picking   53

Module 7 Additional Training Lessons   55
Lesson 31:   Music Theory basics   55
Lesson 32:   Improvise within a song   56
Lesson 33:   Learning solos from recordings   58
Lesson 34:   Ear training tips   60
Lesson 35:   Chord progressions to solo over   62

Lead Guitar Wizardry Conclusion   65

Lead Guitar Wizardry Training Quiz   67

** This book is dedicated to my parents who gave me the patience and work ethic to succeed in life and to my students who allowed me the opportunity to come into their lives and help them to become better guitar players while having fun in the process. In doing so they have helped me to become a better teacher and guitar player. For this I will always be grateful.**

Module 1: Lead guitar basics

Lesson 1: Introduction to notation

When it comes to reading sheet music, tablature will be best for our purposes it is easier to understand and designed specifically for guitar players.

the six tab lines represent the strings with the biggest string on the bottom. Which will be your sixth string or thickest string and is notated as such.

By using this style of notation, it will make learning how to read sheet music a lot easier which will make our ability to learn a lot faster.

In addition to being able to recognize the guitar strings in the tablature we also want to make sure we have a very well-versed understanding of our musical alphabet. Which is listed below.

A A# B C C# D D# E F F# G G# These 12 notes will make up the foundation of everything that we are going to learn in this training guide. And anything that has to do with music on any instrument. So make sure that you take some time to learn and memorize these notes.

These notes will make up the foundational properties of all of the magic and wizardry that we are going to create to become a great guitarist. No matter if we are working on being lead guitar wizards, rhythm guitar alchemists or both.

Now once we have determined that we know our musical alphabet, we recognize the lines on the guitar in the tablature, we are now ready to understand how we recognize frets and the lines of the strings that they reside on. The following examples will show this.

This indicates the third fret on the first string.

This indicates the sixth fret on the fourth string.

This indicates the fifth fret on the sixth string.

When playing a string without putting a finger on the fretboard this is considered open. And this will be indicated by a zero on a line as shown in the example below.

This indicates that you will play the sixth string without putting your finger on the fretboard. This is considered "open" and is used throughout this training manual.

Here is an example of multiple notes on one string that would be played one right after another.

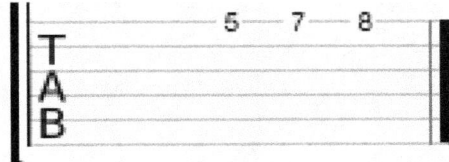

This indicates that you play the fifth, seventh & eighth notes on the first string.

Sometimes when reading tablature, there will be notes or symbols underneath the tablature that will indicate changes in rhythm & timing.

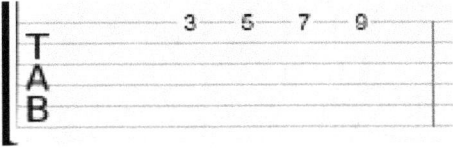

Count   1+ 2 + 3 + 4

These numbers and symbols indicate time value. In this example it will be one and two and three and four. That would be the timing that you would play the above four notes on the 1st string.

This is not always indicated in tablature, especially with songs you find on the net. But it's still best to understand how this works so when you do come across it when reading sheet music.

These kind of fretboard diagrams are helpful in being able to visualize chord shapes, patterns, techniques, concepts and many other things that are related to learning guitar. Whether that be rhythm or lead.

Lesson 2: 12 Bar Progression.

The 12 bar progression is a chord sequence of three chords that play in a pattern of 12 bars or measures. This a very common progression used in blues and rock. It is a great place to start for playing solos over.

Why?

Because your ear (whether you realize it or not) recognizes this chord progression. And the reason for this is because it's very common in a lot of songs.

If you listen to any type of rock within the last 30 years you're going to see many many songs that utilize this progression in many different keys.

Here is an example of 12 bar blues in A:

A

D   A

E   D   A   E

6

As you can clearly see from the diagram, the three chords in this progression are played within 12 measures hence the term 12 bar or 12 bar blues.

This is the rhythm type we're going to start learning how to play lead guitar over and once we learn this we're going to learn how to utilize it over other keys as well. Because if you can do it in one key, you can do it in all keys.

When it comes to playing melody, lead guitarists use the technique of playing riffs (single note rhythms) over the progression that repeat in unison throughout the piece of music.

These riffs are great because they help you to develop timing and ear training. As well as the ability to listen to where you should be in relationship to the chords being played beneath the lead guitar riff.

This exercise is essential for being a good lead guitarist. You must always know where you're at in relation to the chord progression and the other musicians you're playing with. Whether that be with live musicians or just recorded songs & backing tracks.

Here is an example of a common type of lead guitar riff:

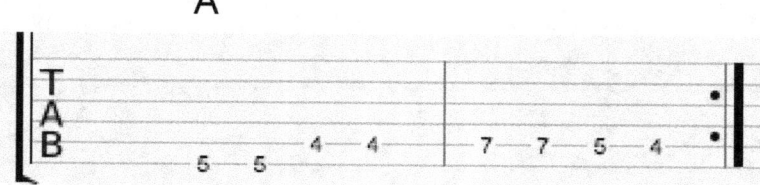

When the progression moves through the chords, you as a lead guitarist must change with it to stay in harmony with the chord changes.

Your guitar riff will be designed to work well within the specific chords timing that is played within the specific key. In this example, the key of A.

The strings that the riff is played on will change but the riff itself will stay the same and match the root note of the chord it is being played over. This is why it is essential to know your notes on the fretboard.

This way you can develop a good understanding of the chords being played in the progression, and you can create a melody line that fits harmonically and diatonically.

Here's an example of this same riff being played on the fifth string.

D

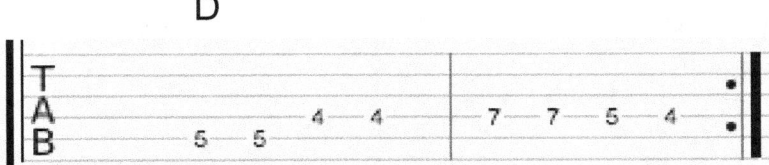

As you can see the riff stays the same it's just the string in which it's played on changes. That's because you want the riff to match the chords that it's being played over.

So in this example when you're on the A chord you want to play on the 6th string at the fifth fret because that it where the A note is located. When you play over the D chord you want to play on the fifth string at the fifth fret because that's where the D note is located.

Here is the example with the E chord

E

```
T|------------------------------------|
A|-------------6--6------9--9--7--6---|
B|---7--7-----------------------------|
```

Now in addition to the riff being played over the chord, on the last measure you do what is called a turn around. This is like an ending that puts you in position to start the riff over.

Here's an example of a three note turn around.

Try putting this all together and listen to how it sounds. Even if you don't have the chords playing underneath you can still get the feel of the riff, and timing of the 12 bar structure. This type of riff can also & sometimes is, played by bass players as well.

This is a very familiar progression in rock music and blues. If you listen to early recordings from the fifties and sixties you can hear this concept in many many songs.

As you continue to work with this progression, you begin to develop your ear for it and recognize it when it appears. This is a great place to start for lead guitar playing. it is where I started and it is suggested you do the same.

Lesson 3: Your Major scale formula and intervals

Next to the chromatic scale (every note on the fretboard) is the major scale. These are notes that are taken out of the chromatic scale that create the Do Ra Me that we are so familiar with. This is a great scale for developing ear training and eye hand coordination.

In each major scale (in any key) there are root notes to be aware of. These notes have the same name as the key they're being played in (example: A) there will be two of these notes per octave (8 sets of notes) Do Ra Me Fa So La Te Do. See the two Do's? Those are the root notes I'm talking about.

If you go through a set of notes & you don't hear this, it's ether not the major scale or your missing something.

Major scale in one octave in A at the fifth fret.

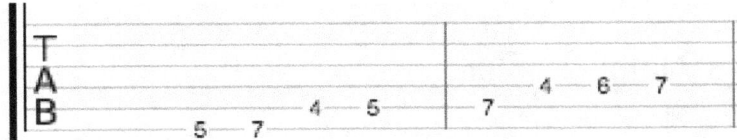

Although I have presented this in A at the fifth fret, you can play it anywhere on the fretboard. Try it at the 8th fret, 10th fret and so on.

This will allow you to have a better understanding of your fretboard as well as develop your ear at the same time. Now remember, it doesn't come overnight but if you work steadily on it you will see progress.

One thing to think about (which is a little insider tip) is that the guitar fretboard can be broken down into patterns and shapes. The more you can remember this, the easier it will be for you to learn.

Intervals

You also want to master what are called intervals. Which is the distance between two notes. These can be broken down into half steps and whole steps. A half step is one fret and a whole step is two frets.

In the previous example, the notes on the sixth string (5 & 7) are a whole step apart (two frets) while the notes on the fifth string (4 & 5) are a half step (one fret) and then you have the 7 on the fifth string which would be another whole step from the 5.

How about the fourth string? Can you figure it out?

Major Scale Formula using whole & half steps.

The interval pattern of the major scale is:

```
1   2   3   4   5   6   7   8  Number value
A   B   C#  D   E   F#  G#  A  Note value
  W   W   H   W   W   W   H    Interval formula
```

Really take some time to look this over & understand it. This will allow you to find notes, what sharps or flats are in any major key & most importantly, how to form chords & progressions to solo over.

This is a "magical" formula you need to master to become a lead guitar wizard. And in doing so, you will not only soar above the crowd but also be able to leave people spellbound with your sacred knowledge of unlocking the "mysteries" of the fretboard.

Lesson 4: Guitar riffs to play over rhythms

In this first example the riff is used throughout the blues progression and utilizes three strings as opposed to two in the last one.

This riff also uses a very common ending. A whole note. Played on the last measure instead of the turnaround that we learned in the previous guitar riff.

A whole note is when you play a note on the first beat only.

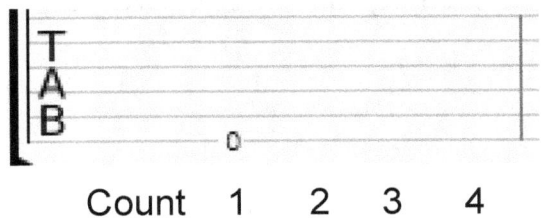

Count 1   2   3   4

As you can see, the note is played on the first beat and held for three.
Riff # 2 example in B:

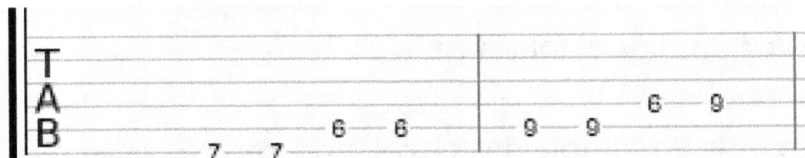

This riff will be played in the key of B because it starts at the 7th fret instead of the 5th. Same concept applies as before in the first riff.

In riff number 3 we are going to utilize ascending and descending notes over three strings. this allows us to increase the length of the riff and bring the notes back down for a different type of sound.

Riff ##3 example in G:

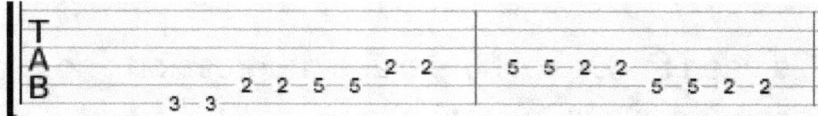

Riff #4 example in G:

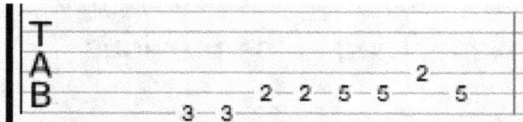

Notice how this riff if very similar to the previous one it just changes on the last two notes. But doesn't continue over two measures. This allows you to create different variations in your riffs.

Riff #5 example in C:

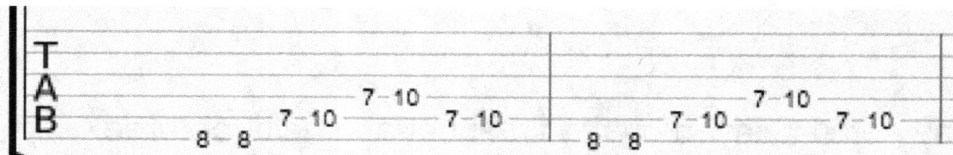

This riff is played over one measure and utilizes three strings. Going up & coming down. This makes for a unique sound as well.

Practice these riff examples until you know them well and can play them over the 12 bar progression by memory. As you do this you will exercise your creativity and come up with more ideas.

These are written in different keys (for example only) but should be played in A over the chords presented in lesson two.

This will allow you to develop dexterity, left/right hand coordination, proper hand positioning, and ear training. Which is needed for a solid lead guitar foundation.

Lesson 5: Alternate picking & octaves

In order to increase your speed and flexibility in your lead playing, you need to master alternate picking. This is the process of picking the strings down and back up.

Alternate picking exercise:

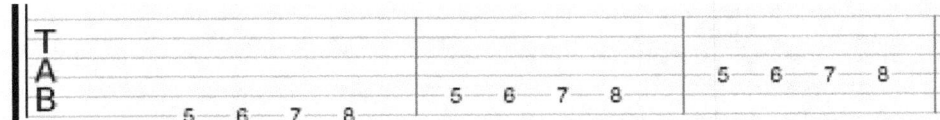

Pick the first note down, second note up. third note down, fourth note up and repeat this process on every string.

Play slow and listen to your notes. Pay close attention to your picking hand for proper placement of your pick & steady timing. Also go back and play the previous riffs learned with this technique.

Be sure to use a four note span using all four fingers. Start around the center of the fretboard. I use frets five through eight because this is a common position to play on the guitar.

This exercise will help to loosen up your fingers. build dexterity, eye hand coordination, ear training and if you know your notes, knowledge in this area as well.

It would be a good idea to work with a metronome or a drum machine that can keep a simple beat. This will help you to develop that internal clock that all guitar players must have.

Major Scale In Two Octaves

In lesson three we learned the major scale in one octave. Do to Do.
Now we are going to look at it in two octaves. This concept will allow you
to learn it on all six strings as well as continued knowledge of the fretboard.

Major scale second octave in A:

If you start with your first octave learned previously you will see very clearly
that you will be able to add this to it with ease.

Once again, practice slowly with down picking then progress to alternate
picking. This will set up your foundation for adding personality to the notes
later in this training guide.

Learning to play riffs over chords and being able to change with the
progression will allow you to stay in key and sound good every time.

Why?

Because you are playing a riff against the chord and playing the same
position as that chord no matter what it is.

Later we will learn how to stay in key even if you don't know what chords
are being played. But for now stick to this approach.

This first section has involved some important fundamental exercises for your lead guitar development. We have covered:

1. Basic guitar riffs and scales.
2. Dexterity and eye-hand coordination.
3. Twelve bar chord progression.
4. The major scale formula.
5. Down and alternate picking.
6. The major scale in two octaves.

Work on this daily and you will set up a good foundation for your development as a lead guitar wizard.

Module 2: Scales & Personality Licks

Lesson 6: Pentatonic scale pattern one.

When it comes to lead guitar wizardry, this is the scale that is most common. It has been used by all the great guitarists. What is great about this scale is it can be used in both major & minor position.

When playing blues & rock it's always a good idea to start off with a minor scale because this gives the style of music a certain sound and emotion.

This scale is derived of five notes that are taken out of the major scale. For example, the notes in the A major scale are:

1 2 3 4 5 6 7 8 (number value)
A B C# D E F# G# A (note value)

Always be aware of your notes in a scale and their number value.
A pentatonic scale:

1 b3 4 5 b7 (number value)
A C D E G (note value)

Notice how we have flattened the three and the seven of the major scale formula. It is these five notes (with two notes that are flattened) that give this scale its sound and character.

We merely start with the major scale formula and take certain notes out of it to create the minor pentatonic scale. Penta meaning 5 and tonic meaning notes. A scale of five notes.

This scale we will call pattern one and start here. There are five of them that span the fretboard and create a "road map" that lets you know where to play. Very much like driving a vehicle.

Once you memorize this pattern & the other four, you will always sound good no matter where you play. So we will start with scale pattern one and it looks like this:

Pattern one in the key of A minor/ C major

I say A minor or C major because this pattern can be used for both keys. Why? Because they are relative. Which means they are made up of the same notes.

This scale is used by all lead guitarists and you should practice it everyday. In different positions along the fretboard until you have it committed to memory.

In doing so we not only learn where to play in this key to sound good, but also increase our musical knowledge that whenever we flatten the third of a major scale or chord it becomes a minor.

In this case of the minor scale we are using for lead guitar playing we also want to flatten the seventh as well. This will give us the sound we're looking for and notes in a pattern sequence that is easy to play.

Always think in patterns. It will allow you to see things on the fretboard you would not normally be able to see. And this will allow you to increase your speed of learning.

Lesson 7: Transposing keys and triplets

When you move this scale to different areas on the fretboard you do what is called transposing. For example, if you play it at the fifth fret it is in A minor. If it is played at the third fret it is G minor and if it is played at the eighth fret it is considered C minor.

That is because this is where these notes are located on the sixth string and are what determine what key you are playing in. So once again, take time to master your notes on your fretboard.

Triplets

Triplets are a series of three notes played in a sequence. These are easy to learn and give us a chance to get to know our pentatonic scale.

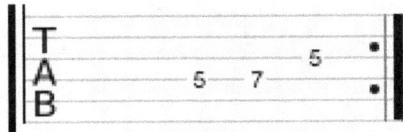

Repeat signs.

If you notice the two dots at the end of the measure, this is a repeat sign. This means to repeat this section of music. Whenever there is two dots in musical notation at the beginning or ending of a section of music, you will repeat this section.

As you can see in the example above, we are to repeat this triplet. This triplet technique when repeated (among others) will add "personality" to the scale and is what makes it and any other scale come alive when you play it.

The note patterns themselves aren't enough. We must learn to add personality to them to make our guitar solos sound interesting to the ear.

So try this technique with other notes in the scale. Work at repeating them just as we have done in the example above. Before you know it, you will be creating your own personality licks. Now let's look at some other ways to do this.

Lesson 8: Hammer ons, pull offs & trills

Next to the triplet we have the hammer on, pull off and trill. These are common techniques of playing a note and either hammering on to it with another finger (hammer on) or pulling a note away with a finger (pull off) or adding the two together repeatedly (trill) and is mastered by all lead guitar wizards.

Hammer on example:

Notice in this example you are adding a note.

Hammer on example 2:

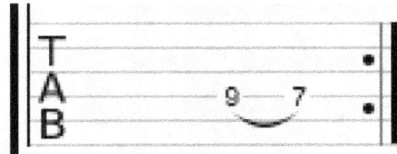

In this example the note is being taken away.

Practice these techniques until you know them very well. Play the first note with your first finger & hammer on or pull off the next note with your third finger.

Hammer ons starts with one finger down, and pull offs starts with two fingers down. Once you have the hammer on & pull off mastered then you can proceed to the trill.

Trill example:

This is when you add the two together and play them repeatedly.

As you progress with mastering these techniques you'll be able to hear them in solos.

If you take time to really work on these techniques and master hearing how they sound in song and how to execute them properly, all I can say is look out world because here you come.

Lesson 9: Bends, slides & vibrato

One of the really cool things about guitar is that it uses a technique that other stringed instruments (piano, violin, ukulele, mandolin etc) don't use and that is the string bend.

Bending strings is essential to learn in lead guitar playing. It is a form of expression that allows you to mimic singing. Just as a person would do with their vocal chords. Your just doing it with your guitar strings.

Bending string example:

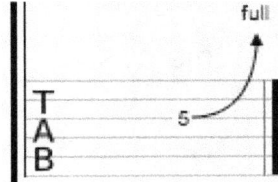

You pick the third string at the fifth fret and bend it up. In this example you would bend up a full step or whole step.

Which of course this can be hard to do when your just starting out. So just bend a little to get used to this technique.

Slides are another common way to get from one note to the next. You pick a note and slide it either up or down the fretboard.

Slide up example:

The slide will be indicated by a diagonal line that in the direction of the slide. In this case you are sliding up to the 7 from the 5.

Slide down example:

As like before, you slide in the direction of the slanted line. In this case down the fretboard from the 7 to the 4.

In addition to the bend & slide we also want to master a technique associated with lead guitar playing that is one of the hardest. This technique is the vibrato.

Vibrato is where you pick a note and vibrate it slightly up and down. This gives the note a vocal-like quality and allows for a very cool expression of your lead guitar playing.

Vibrato example:

This is indicated by a wavy line above the note.

Executing proper vibrato is one of the hardest things to do correctly on guitar. In my experience, I've seen many people struggle with this technique.

But if you practice this and all these other techniques individually until you know them really well you'll create some awesome sounds with your guitar.

Now let's look at some examples that will teach us how to put them together so we can sound like a lead guitar wizard.

Lesson 10: Combining Techniques

By this time we have learned a few "tricks" of the trade. We've learned about picking, scales, triplets, hammer ons, pull offs, bends, slides, vibrato & trills.

Now we want to combine these ingredients to create interesting phrases that sound like music. These techniques (among others) are tools that you will use in your lead guitar craftsmanship to weave magic that will leave your audience spellbound.

In these examples we will stay in the key of A but be sure to try them in other places on the fretboard so that you get familiar with how they sound in different keys.

Example 1:

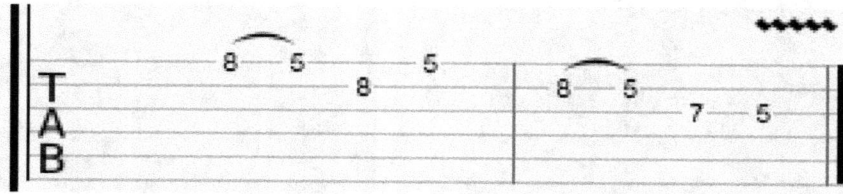

Example 2:

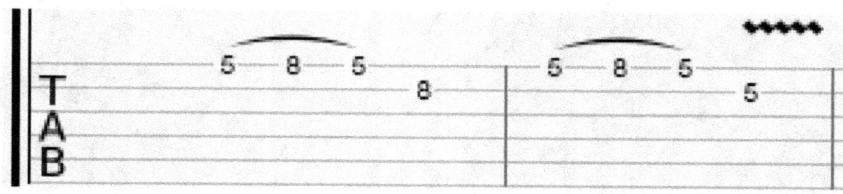

Example 3:

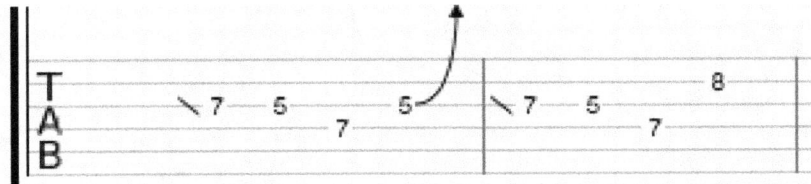

Example 4:

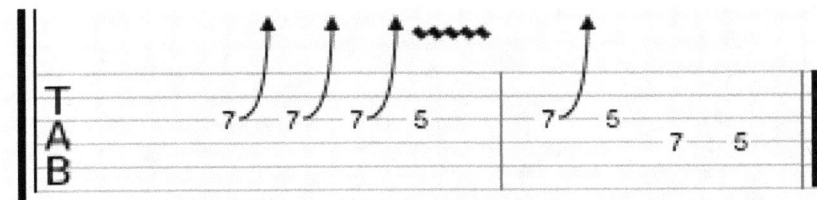

Example 5:

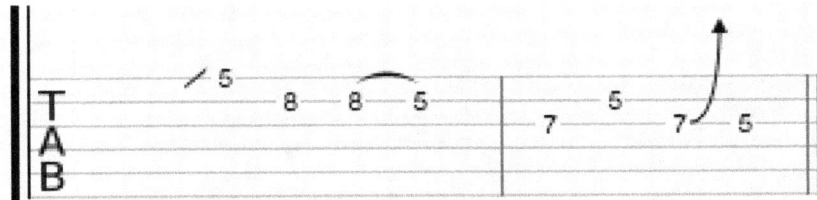

When practicing these techniques on the middle strings (D & G) work at barring your index finger across the fretboard for two reasons:

1. Makes it easier to execute on these strings.
2. It helps to mute unwanted notes. Which helps with controlling string vibration and clarity in tone.

Practice these lick examples all over the fretboard. Not just where they are written. This will help for technique recognition & ear training of different sounds along the fretboard.

Module 3: Key Progressions & Blues Scale

Lesson 11: Pattern one extended notes

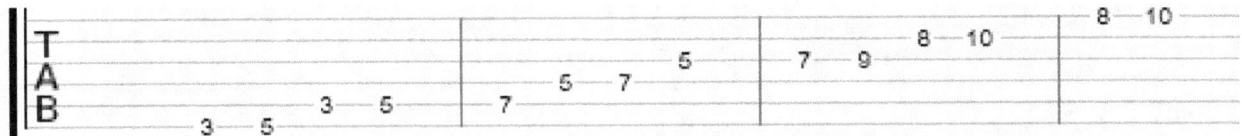

By adding notes to pattern 1 from other patterns (5 in all) you extend the life of the notes. You also get more familiar with the note location on the fretboard.

Always be practicing visualization! You must be able to "see" the notes on the fretboard. This will allow for faster finger placement and note location retention.

Extended notes are a good way to practice your sliding technique. Here are a few examples.

Example 1:

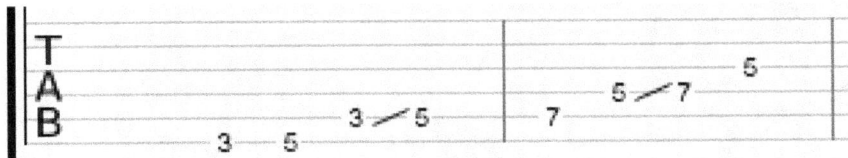

Example 2:

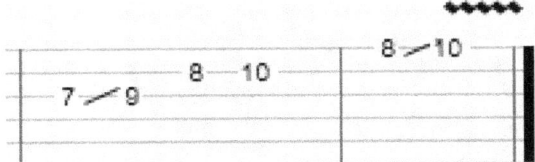

Example 3:

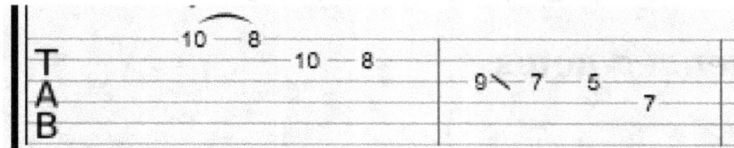

Example 4:

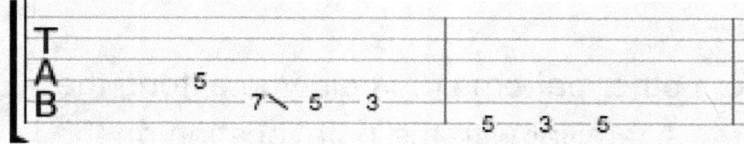

Use finger pressure to make sure your finger stays in contact with the fretboard when you slide. It will seem a bit uncomfortable at first sliding over the fretwire but in time this will go away.

Sliding is a prime technique for playing lead guitar & these extended notes work well with sliding up & down the fretboard.

Make sure to practice sliding up & down. Listen to the notes & how they sound when sliding into or out of them and be sure to memorize these extended notes.

Lesson 12: Major pentatonic scale

What is great about the major pentatonic scale is that it is the exact same notes as the minor pentatonic. You just start on a different note within the scale.

For instance, since A minor is relative to C major (because they consist of the same notes) you can play this same scale in both keys.

If your playing in A minor, you would start at the fifth fret on the 6th string (A) and if you were playing in C major you could use the same scale, you would just start on the 8th fret because this is where the C note is.

A minor pentatonic:

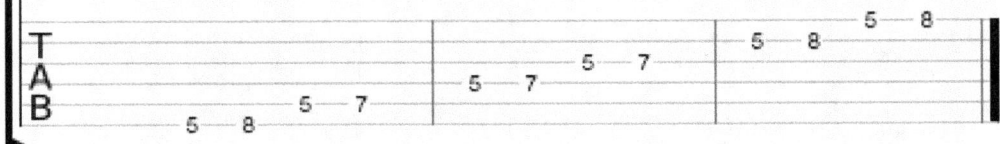

C Major pentatonic:

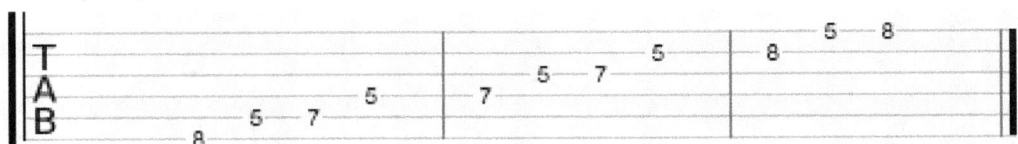

As you can clearly see, the notes are the same it's just what order you play them in & what note you start on that makes the difference.

One secret to remember is that the relative minor to any major is located 3 frets down on the fretboard. For example, the C is located at the 8th fret. It's relative minor is the A which is located three frets down.

So if your playing in A major, what is its relative minor? If your playing in D major, what is its relative minor that is located three frets down?

This technique works with any note located on the fretboard. Try finding these relative majors & minors throughout the guitar and increase your fretboard knowledge.

Now that you know what notes to play over any major or minor progression, you can now work on how to use them, where they are located and how you can benefit from their execution.

Lesson 13: Minor key progressions

Most songs in rock are written in minor key progressions. Some are written in major, but most in minor. The reason for this is because it gives the songs their sound. And since rock is derived from blues, it is mostly written in they key.

Minor key progression example #1
Am / / / / G / / / / F / / / / E7 / / / /
The slashes represent the beat. Four per each chord.

With this chord progression you can play the pattern one scale at the fifth fret & it will sound great. You can also play over this progression at the 17th fret because in this position, the notes are the same.

If you were playing over a G minor progression, you would play this scale pattern at the third fret because that is where G is located on the 6th string.

By knowing where notes are located on the fretboard on all six strings, you are going to expand your lead guitar playing to the max. Because knowing "what" to play on the fretboard is key number one. Knowing "where" to play is key number two.

Take some time to wrap this concept around your brain. It might take a while but if you work at it you'll get it with ease. Here are a few more simple examples to look at:

Minor key example #2
Gm //// Cm //// Dm //// Cm ////

Minor key example #3
Bm //// Em //// F#m //// Bm ////

Minor key progression #4
Em //// Am //// Bm //// Em ////

Minor key example #5
Cm //// Fm //// Gm //// Cm ////

Minor key example #6
Dm //// Gm //// Am //// Dm ////

These are very common minor chord progressions in rock & roll music. You can hear these in multitudes of songs throughout the decades since rock was first born. Back when Elvis, Little Richard, Chuck Berry & Jerry Lee Lewis caused people to go crazy with this new sound.

It is still widely used in rock music today and any guitar player playing this style of music, no matter if they are playing rhythm or lead should be familiar with these progressions.

These progressions come from rhythm & blues and will always sound good no matter what century they are being played in. They represent the foundation for rock & roll music and playing lead guitar solos.

So make sure you know these minor key progressions. For they will serve you well on your journey to becoming a great lead guitar wizard. That is provided you develop the commitment & discipline to do so.

If you take the time necessary you will not only learn to understand and play the techniques, but you will also develop the most crucial element of them all.

Self confidence!!!

And that my friend is priceless!

Lesson 14: Tremolo picking

By this time in our studies we should have a pretty good grasp of how to play and where to play on the fretboard using some basic techniques. By mastering these fundamentals, you'll be able to play against any chord progression in any key and sound good in the process.

In addition to all this you can now start working on tremolo picking. This will help you to develop speed and accuracy.

When practicing your alternate picking, You'll notice over time you'll get faster. When you get faster and can pick consistently then you'll be able to tremolo pick. Which is rapid alternate picking.

This technique involves rapid hand movement On any given note on any given string. And produces a very unique sound that is common to lead guitar Wizardry.

You hold the pick close to the strings (anchor the pinky to the guitar body if need be) and practice going through the scales you've learned while you execute alternate picking. Slow at first, but speed up over time.

It is this speeding up over time that turns your alternate picking into tremolo picking. And to get down fast solos you will need to take time to master this valuable technique.

Tremolo picking example #1

This tells us that we rapidly pick the 5th fret on the first string.

Tremolo picking example #2

In this example we rapidly pick the 12th fret on the first string.

Try doing this elsewhere on other frets and other strings. This technique is going to allow you to produce some really neat musical phrases that'll sound freakin awesome!

Lesson 15: The Blues scale

Next we will learn the blues scale. We learn this next because it is almost the same scale as the pentatonic. The only difference is that it adds a note to the scale in two different places to create a more darker sad sound.

The note that we will add to the scale is the flat 5th. This note is very important to know in any key because by adding or subtracting this note, is going to change the "mood & emotion" of the music.

Blues scale in A

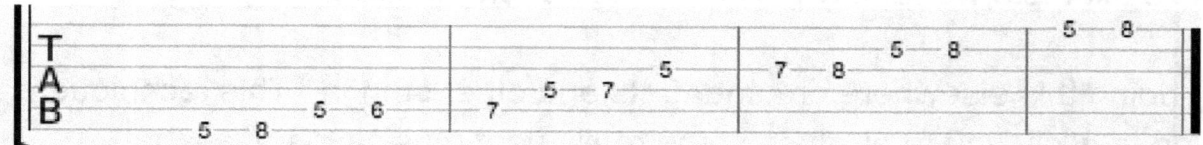

As you can see, we've added two notes to the pentatonic scale. One at the 6th fret fifth string and one at the 8th fret third string.

This is actually the same note, just presented in two different positions. It gives the scale a different sound and allows for the artist (you) to create a different mood & emotion.

This example is presented at the fifth fret but see if you can add these notes to the scale in other positions on the fretboard. Listen to how it sounds with and without these added notes.

Being able to know what note this is and adding it to the scale in any key is what your shooting for. But this can only be done through study & practice.

Module 4: Additional Pentatonic Scale patterns

Lesson 16 Pentatonic Scale Pattern Two

All these scale patterns will be written in the key of A at the fifth fret. Move them around the fretboard to really know them well in other keys.

This scale starts where pattern one ends on the eighth fret.

Lesson 17: Pentatonic Scale Pattern Three

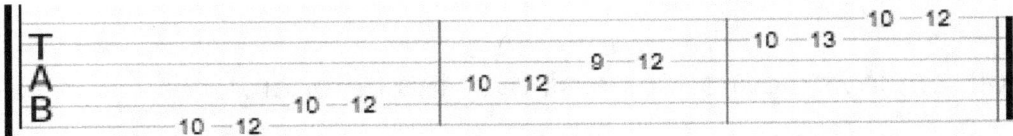

This scale starts where pattern two ends on the tenth fret.

Lesson 18: Pentatonic Scale Pattern Four

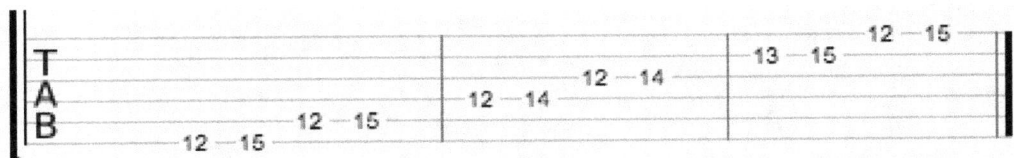

This scale starts where pattern three ends on the twelfth fret.

Lesson 19: Pentatonic Scale Pattern Five

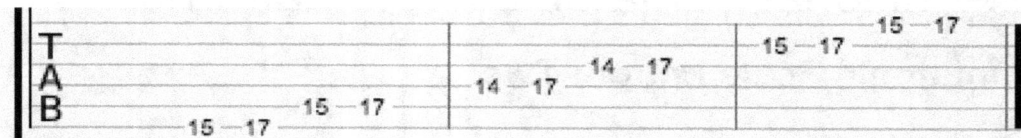

This scale starts where pattern four ends on the fifteen fret.

When going through all five patterns you should end up back at pattern one on the 17th fret. Which will start the process all over again. If you do not end up on the 17th fret, go back and figure out why.

If you can grasp this concept and be able to connect all five patterns along the guitar fretboard, you will be able to play solos in any key at any fret and sound good every single time.

That is the magic of playing guitar solos all over the fretboard!

Lesson 20: Summary Of All Five Pentatonic Scales

These five scale patterns will set a solid foundation for your lead guitar playing. These are scale patterns that are used by all the great guitar players. Jimi Hendrix, Jimmy Page, Eric Clapton, Stevie Ray, Angus Young, Van Halen, Randy Rhoads and countless others.

So take some time and study these. Really get to know them. Practice them daily. One scale at a time until you can visualize them on your fretboard. See how they all connect with each other like puzzle pieces and allow you to span the entire fretboard.

With these five scales and all the little spells & incantations that you have learned so far (bends, slides, vibrato etc.) you should be able to pull off some pretty awesome lead guitar magic.

Module 5: Scales With Additional Notes

Lesson 21: Blues Scale With Additional Notes

If you add even more notes to the scale as passing tones (notes you play but don't necessarily land on) this will allow you to create more diversity in your playing. They will allow you to add more color and emotion.

Blues Scale With additional notes Example:

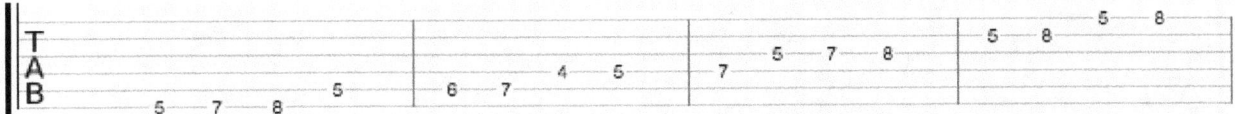

Lesson 22: Major Pentatonic Scale With Additional Notes

The major pentatonic scale contains the 1 2 3 5 and 6 of the major scale. As additional notes the 4 and 7 can be added to complete the major scale. Remember when playing major key scales always be shooting for the Do Rae Me sound.

Major Pentatonic scale with additional notes Example

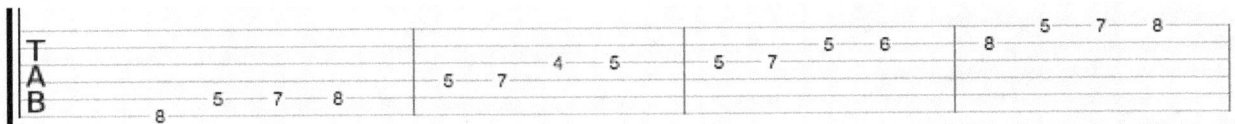

This is the major scale in two octaves. Become familiar with this and how to find the notes. As you further your study of the scale patterns the fretboard starts to become more complex.

Lesson 23: Minor Pentatonic Scale With Additional Notes

As we have learned in previous lessons, the major and minor pentatonic scale are the same just where you decide to start is what changes.

In this example we will add a few extra notes to the minor scale starting at the fifth fret instead of the eighth.

Minor pentatonic scale with additional notes example.

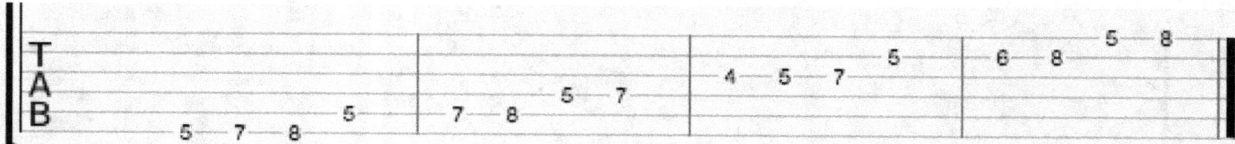

By adding some extra notes as passing tones to the scale, we are now able to expand what we create within the same guidelines of the scale.

Lesson 24: Finger Dexterity Development

As you begin to stretch out the scales you will notice that using all your fingers will help with your speed and dexterity. So in this lesson we are going to look at some simple exercises that can help you to develop this skill.

Example 1.

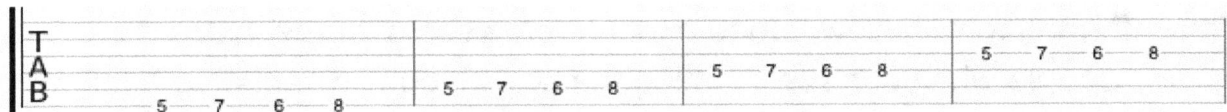

Example 2.

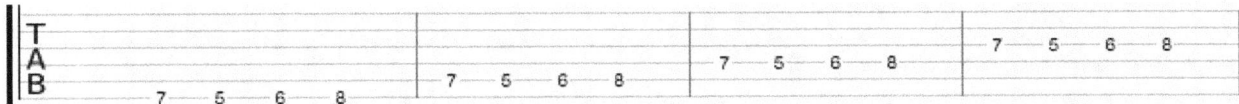

Example 3.

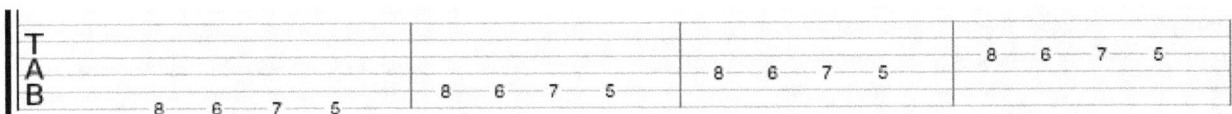

Example 4.

Example 5.

These 5 examples should be practiced every day. They provide each finger to lead the progression individually which will allow for better dexterity.

I recommend you also practice both down and alternate picking as this will help to gain control and speed in your playing. Be disciplined in your study. Don't take this lightly.

This information will allow you to execute prowess over the instrument and amaze people with your spell casting magic. Which is what being a lead guitar wizard is all about.

Lesson 25: Finger Tapping and Repeated Licks

One of the all time cool things to do on the guitar is finger tap. This where you do a hammer-on with one finger and tap with your other or tap with both fingers. There are many different ways you can do this and through experimentation you will be able to discover more. But here are a couple examples to get you started.

Finger tap example 1:

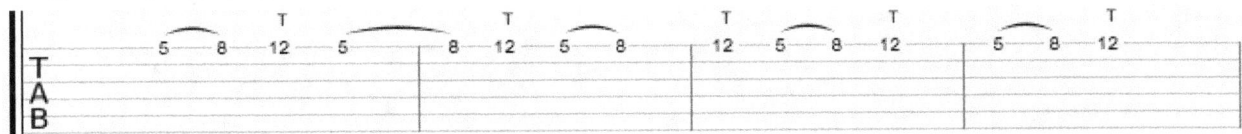

In this example you do a hammer-on with one finger and tap with the other.

Finger tap example 2:

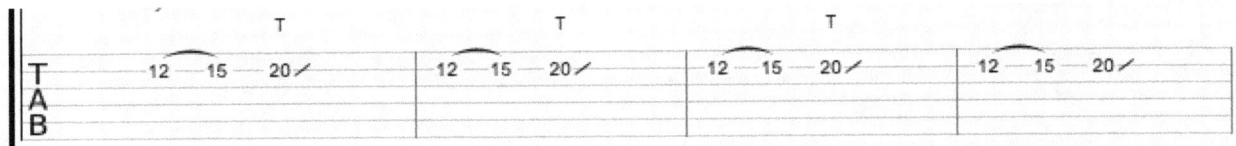

In this example you tap with both fingers. I usually use my index fingers for this type of tapping.

Finger tap example 3:

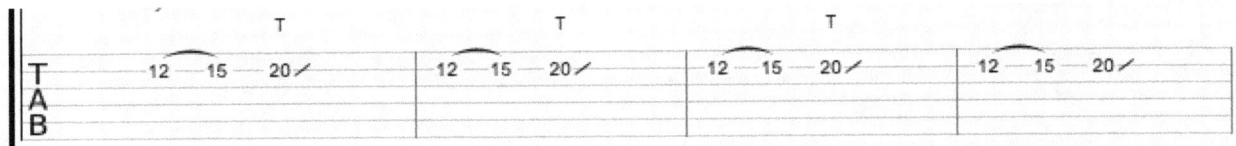

In this example you hammer-on and tap like example 1, but this time you add a slide up the fretboard. Listen to how cool this sounds.

These are just a few examples on how you can approach the art of finger tapping and repeated licks. There is plenty more to discover, but just

Mastering these three different techniques will allow you to create some jaw-dropping sounds that when done correctly, will amaze your listeners.

This is a technique that was made famous by Eddie Van Halen. Who once said in an interview that he used to practice up to 12 hours a day.

Can you believe that? Just listen to some of his solos on his first album. I think you'll see very clearly what I'm talking about when it comes to the commitment and dedication required to become a lead guitar wizard.

Module 6: Harmony, Octaves, Hybrid, Sweep picking

Lesson 26: Harmony Notes In 3rds

Harmony notes are two notes played together you can use in both rhythm and lead guitar playing. The most common are 3rds and 6ths and can be used to make all kinds of cool sounds. Thirds are consisted of the 1 & 3rd of the major scale.

For example, in the key of C the two notes would be the C & E. In the key of D the two notes would be D & F. Key of A would be A & C#. Find the third in all scales and then learn to play them together on two strings. Like the second and third strings.

Example in thirds

```
T----5----6----8----10-----|--12---13---15---17--
A----5----7----9----10-----|--12---14---16---17--
B--------------------------|---------------------
```

In this example the root note (the one) is on the lower string and the third is on the higher string. Try this out in other keys.

Lesson 27: Harmony notes in 6ths

In thirds we found the note was below the root (the 1 of the scale) on the second string, but for 6th's we find the note is located above the root on the fourth string 7th fret. Remember, in these harmony notes your going to use the 1 & 6 of the major scale.

In C it would be the C and A. In G it would be the G and E. Find these notes just as you did with the thirds. Same concept just use the sixth note instead of the third note of the major scale.

Thirds with a string in between.

```
T|---1---3---5---6----|---8---10--12--13---|
A|---2---3---5---7----|---9---10--12--14---|
B|--------------------|--------------------|
```

When you skip a string, it allows you to use hybrid picking. This technique uses the pick and finger together to create a different type of sound.

Make sure to always go through your notes on your fretboard to get familiar with where they are located. Since there is a string between these two notes you can add some diversity to your playing.

You can pick both notes individually or use a pick and your finger to play both notes together. This is a common technique in lead guitar playing and will be looked at further in the next couple lessons.

Lesson 28: Harmony With Octaves.

In addition to your thirds & sixths, you can also use octaves to create some very cool magical spells. Same concept as before but here you use the 1 & 8 of the scale. Basically, two notes that are the same just a pitch apart.

Harmony in Octaves Example

```
T|----6----8----10----11----|----13----15----17----18----|
A|----3----5----7-----8-----|----10----12----14----15----|
B|--------------------------|----------------------------|
```

As you can see, the notes are a string apart like the sixths. So you can use the same approach as before. You just use different notes. This is why it is important to know your notes.

Find these on multiple strings and see how they work well together. Understand why they work, where they are located and how they are utilized to your benefit.

Lesson 29: Hybrid Picking.

Hybrid picking is when you use both your fingers and your pick. This technique allows you to create some interesting sounds that you would not be able to create with just a pick or with just your fingers.

With the 3rds, siths & octaves you can utilize this concept quite well. You use the pick for the lower note and use one of your fingers for the higher note.

Hybrid Picking Example

```
T|----------------------|------------------------|
A|---2---3---5---7------|---9---10--12--14-------|
B|---3---5---7---8------|--10---12--14--15-------|
```

In this example you can play the strings together or individually. It's really up to you. Be creative. Try out different fingers and different approaches.

Work at finding your notes on all your strings and which ones belong in each key. This will take some time but to be a great lead guitar wizard, you must know the ingredients to your spells and incantations and know which ones go together to cast the kind of musical magic you choose to create.

Lesson 30: Sweep Picking.

This is a unique technique where all the notes on the strings are picked downward up the scale and back upward down the scale in a sweeping motion.

This creates a rapid up & down motion with the pick hand. Start slow to get the technique down and speed up gradually.

Example #1

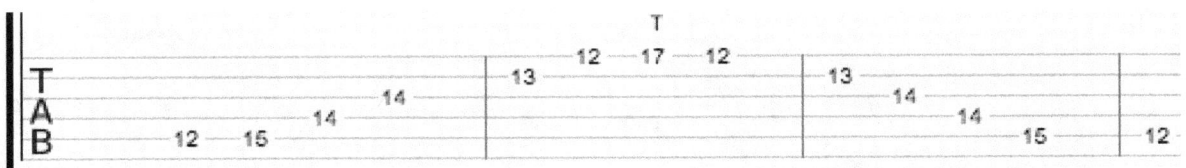

Pick down in one motion to the 12, tap on the 17, then back up to the 12 in a sweeping motion.

Example #2

Same as before except in this example you are going in the opposite direction with the notes. But the technique is the same.

The objective of this technique is to make it sound like all notes are picked as one. Very quickly. As if you were sweeping a broom across the floor. That is why it's called sweep picking.

54

Module 7: Additional Training Lessons

Lesson 31: Music Theory Basics

All music is based on the 12 notes in the musical alphabet.
A A# B C C# D D# E F F# G # Study these notes and know them like the back of your hand. This is considered the Chromatic Scale.

Out of the Chromatic Scale we can create the Major Scale. Which is the 8 notes that make up the Do Ra Me that is so well known. We take these notes form the chromatic scale and create all 7 Major Scales.

Do Ra Me Fa So La Te Do. Syllables for the Major Scale.
Example: G Major: G A B C D E F# G
         A Major: A B C# D E F# G# A
         C Major: C D E F G A B C

There are 8 notes in all major scales that are taken out of the chromatic scale which is all the notes in the musical alphabet. The major and minor scales (all scales actually) can be broken down into a scientific formula which consist of whole steps and half steps.

Once you can decipher these formulas and intervals like a scientist, you will be able to find which sharps or flats are in each key and any note in the scale. This will allow you to be able to mix and match notes to create any kind of magic you choose. Very powerful stuff!!

Major formula W-W-H-W-W-W-H-W
Minor formula W-H-W-W-H-W-W
W= whole step, two frets and H=half step, 1 fret.

Lesson 32: Improvise Within a Song

Most guitar solos you hear on record can either be improvised on the spot or can be methodically worked out. Some players create on the spot and record what comes out at the time (spontaneous combustion) while others sit down and create different ideas (methodical phrasing) and then either combine them or choose which one is the best.

In this lesson we will look at the former of the two. Improvisation. Very much like a comedian who just makes up stuff on the spot. As a lead guitar wizard you will need to hone your skills at improvising within a song. You will need to know what to play and where to play it.

The information learned in the previous 30 lessons will allow you to do that. But you must be diligent in your practice and study. You must know your materials very well to be able to create on the fly.

Here are a few ideas that can help you in this area:

1. Know your notes on all six strings throughout the fretboard.
2. Know exactly where all your keys are located. This can be done on the sixth string for all keys.
3. Know your pentatonic major and minor scales to the point you can visualize them on the fretboard. See how they connect together in any key.
4. Know how to execute all your personality techniques (hammer-ons, pull-offs, bends, slides, vibrato etc)
5. Know how to play guitar riffs against chord progressions in all keys.

These are just a few of the things that can help you improvise a solo on the spot and amaze people with your musical knowledge. But it really comes down to practice!

You must put in the practice time to really understand these concepts and be able to put them into practical application. Without that you will only know them in theory.

And although having knowledge of any kind is beneficial in theory, in guitar playing it is essential that you be able to put it into performance.

Lesson 33: Learning Solos From Recordings

This is a very important skill to know and be able to execute if you are to become a lead guitar wizard. All great guitar players previously mentioned developed the ability to do this and you must too.

That is why it is good to learn how to read the written word. This will allow you to see insights unknown to most (because they can't read the written word and don't want to take the time to learn) and allow you to develop your ear.

Being able to duplicate solos as they are written is an advanced skill and requires much discipline. Develop this discipline and you will be able to do things most guitar players can't. Not to mention the fun of playing solos from your favorite artists who inspire you to play in the first place.

Here are a few tips to develop this skill:

1. Start out with something simple. Like a Beatles tune. George Harrison has some nice tasty solos that are easy to start out on. But if you don't like the Beatles, then try a simple solo from a player you like. Go through their songs and find one that's simple.

2. See if you can find the tabs on it and look into what techniques are being used (bends, slides, etc) and practice these individually to get familiar with the sounds that are being produced. Then proceed to learn the melody.

3. Once you have the melody (solo) down all the way through, then try to play it with the song. This will be difficult at first, but as you work at it you will get better, it will get easier and you will start to see how you have accomplished something special.

4. Once you get to this point repeat the process with another solo. Keep a binder of your solos so you can come back to them at a later time and keep refreshing your memory. This will allow you to refer to them at a later time if need be.

5. Be disciplined in your study & practice. Have patience with your learning for this is a skill not all guitar players can do and it takes the most skilled and disciplined craftsman to do this job. Look at yourself as a craftsman who knows his tools and knows how to use them to the very best of their ability.

6. It is also a good idea to use a phrase trainer to slow down the solo if it is too fast and be able to loop certain musical passages for easier and quicker learning. For some solos from professional lead guitar wizards can be a bit complicated and quick on the draw. So tools like these can be very useful and beneficial to your overall learning.

With today's modern technology this can be done quite easily. I used to have to learn from cassette tapes and CD's. Play, stop, rewind. Play, stop, rewind. Play, stop, rewind.

It's much easier today, but still the same process. That is why you have to have be disciplined and committed to the craft. Or you just won't get through the work.

Lesson 34: Ear Training

Being able to translate what you hear to the guitar without looking at sheet music is what's called ear training. This is the way most guitar players approach learning. They sit down, listen to a piece of music and then proceed to pick out the notes.

This is another great technique to learn and time should be spent on it as well. And once some time is spent doing this you will be able to develop not only your ear, but also your confidence.

Here are a few tips in the area of ear training:

1. Play a scale very slowly through one octave. As you go try to sing along wit the notes and match the pitch the best you can.

2. Play one note and try to match it with your voice. Continue doing this until you are confident you are singing each note correctly.

3. Hum along to simple melodies (like the beatles or anything from the 50's is good) and then try to duplicate them on your guitar. Then play with the song to judge your results.

4. Play the root note of a scale and then try to hum or sing the rest of the scale and judge if it sounds correct. If so, check it by playing the scale on the guitar.

5. Continue to do the above exercises until you begin to see results. It's best to try to sing. It really helps out with developing this skill. But if you don't feel comfortable singing, then just hum the note.

Ear training takes time to develop so be sure to have patience and don't get discouraged if it comes slowly. It will eventually develop you just have to stick with it long enough to see results. How long? That depends on you.

If you decide to put in a lot you'll get out a lot. If you decide to skim over parts and only learn what comes easy you will not get good results overall.

When it comes to training your ear, it takes time and effort and it is not easy. So if you decide to do so, take your time and develop the skills necessary.

Lesson 35: Chord Progressions To Solo Over.

Progression #1

| G | Em | C | D |

Progression #2

| C | Em | F | G |

Progression #3

| A | D | E | A |

Progression # 4

| E | G | A | B |

Progression #5

| C | A# | G# | G |

Use these progressions to practice soloing over. Trying out licks and note placement. Try to figure out what key you're in and what notes are necessary to play within it.

As I've stated before, learning to play lead guitar and being able to execute it well takes the most serious commitment to the instrument. More than average hours of dedicated study and practice.

Put in the time and see how you will discover things within yourself that you never knew existed. See your guitar skills blossom into something cool and wonderful.

64

Lead Guitar Wizardry Conclusion.

If you've reached it to here congratulations! You should now have a well developed foundation for playing lead guitar and becoming a lead guitar wizard.

Someone who knows their tools, techniques and an understanding of how to create awesome lead guitar magic. As stated before, you want to be like a craftsman.

Know your materials intimately and be aware of all the possibilities inherent in them. If there is anything you don't understand, be sure to go back through the lesson until you do. You will find some lessons will come to you faster than others. This is normal.

I can't begin to tell you how many of these lessons have come to me the hard way. But with commitment, dedication and consistent practice I got through them and I know you will too.

This will conclude our lessons on lead guitar wizardry volume 1. Good luck in your studies. Thanks for taking the time to read this and hopefully, you've took action on the lessons and are now much better then when you started.

Use the additional blank pages to take notes and work out musical formulas, concepts and techniques to make sure you fully understand the material.

Lead Guitar Wizardry Training Quiz

See how well you know the fundamentals of being a lead guitar wizard.

Lesson 1.

Q: What is notation?
A: _____

Q: What 12 notes make up the musical alphabet?
A: _____

Q: What indicates time value?
A: _____

Lesson 2.

Q: What is a 12 bar progression?
A: _____

Q: What are single note rhythms called?
A: _____

Q: These are very familiar in what styles of music?
A: _____

Lesson 3.

Q: What is the major scale formula?
A: _____

Q: What are intervals?
A: _____

Q: What are whole steps and half steps?
A: _____

Lesson 4.

Q: What kind of note is played on the first beat only?
A: _____

Q: What 3 keys are presented in this lesson?
A: _____

Q: What will this allow you to develop?
A: _____

Lesson 5.

Q: What do you need to master to increase your speed?
A: _____

Q: What tools are useful for building your internal clock?
A: _____

Q: What in this lesson is presented in two octaves?
A: _____

Lesson 6.

Q: What is the most common scale in lead guitar playing?
A: _____

Q: How many notes is this scale made up of?
A: _____

Q: Why is this essential to know?
A: _____

Lesson 7.

Q: What is transposing?
A: _____

Q: What are triplets?
A: _____

Q: What do two dots at the end of a section of music mean?
A: _____

Lesson 8.

Q: What is a hammer on?
A: _____

Q: What is a pull off?
A: _____

Q: What is a trill?
A: _____

Lesson 9.

Q: What are bends?
A: _____

Q: What are slides?
A: _____

Q: What does vibrato mean?
A: _____

Lesson 10.

Q: Why bar your index finger across the fretboard?
A: _____

Q: Why combine techniques?
A: _____

Q: How will this affect your audience?
A: _____

Lesson 11.

Q: Why add notes to pattern one?
A: _____

Q: Extended notes are good for practicing what?
A: _____

Q: A minor is relative to what major?
A: _____

Lesson 12.

Q: What is great about the major pentatonic scale?
A: _____

Q: The relative minor to any key is located where?
A: _____

Q: What separates the major from the minor pentatonic scale?
A: _____

Lesson 13.

Q: Most songs in rock are written in what key progression?
A: _____

Q. What do / / / / represent in the music notation?
A: _____

Q: What fret would you play the scale pattern in the key of G minor?
A: _____

Lesson 14.

Q: What is tremolo picking?
A: _____

Q: What will this technique help you develop?
A: _____

Q: Tremolo evolves from what type of other picking?
A: _____

73

Lesson 15.

Q: What is the blues scale?
A: _____

Q: What note is added to the blues scale?
A: _____

Q: What kind of sound difference does this scale make?
A: _____

Lesson 16.

Q: What is the pattern # taught in this lesson?
A: _____

Q: Why learn it?
A: _____

Lesson 17.

Q: What is the pattern # taught in this lesson?
A: _____

Q: Why learn it?
A: _____

Lesson 18.

Q: What is the pattern # taught in this lesson?
A _____

Q: Why Learn it?
A: _____

Lesson 19.

Q: What pattern # is taught in this lesson?
A: _____

Q: Why learn it?
A: _____

Lesson 20.

Q: What does learning lessons 16-19 accomplish?
A: _____

Q: What is needed to be done with these on the fretboard?
A: _____

Q: What should you be able to accomplish by now.
A: _____

Lesson 21.

Q: What kind of notes are played but not necessarily landed on?
A: _____

Q: What will they allow you to do?
A: _____

Lesson 22.

Q: The major pentatonic scale contains what notes of the major scale?
A: _____

Q: What notes can be added?
A: _____

Q: What sound are you shooting for when playing the major scale?
A: _____

Q: What starts to happen as you study the scale patterns?
A: _____

Lesson 23.

Q: What are we able to do as we add extra notes to the scale?
A: _____

Q: What can be benefited from doing this?
A: _____

Lesson 24.

Q: What will help you to develop your dexterity in this lesson?
A: _____

Q: What kind of picking is recommended in this lesson?
A: _____

Q: What benefit will we get from this?
A: _____

Lesson 25.

Q: What is finger tapping?
A: _____

Q: What techniques are utilized to execute it?
A: _____

Q: Who made this type of technique famous?
A: _____

Lesson 26.

Q: What are harmony notes?
A: _____

Q: What type are taught in this lesson?
A: _____

Lesson 27.

Q: What type are taught in this lesson?
A: _____

Q: What is different about these type of harmony notes?
A: _____

Lesson 28.

Q: What additional notes can be used in this manner?
A: _____

Q: What notes are used in these type of harmony notes?
A: _____

Lesson 29.

Q; What is hybrid picking?
A: _____

Q: What can you utilize this concept with?
A: _____

Q: What is a must to know to create with this technique?
A: _____

Lesson 30.

Q: What is sweep picking?
A: _____

Q: What does this create with the picking hand?
A: _____

Q: What is the main objective to this technique?
A: _____

Lesson 31.

Q: All music is based on what?
A: _____

Q: The major scale is created out of what scale?
A: _____

Q: Why is it important to know the major and minor scale formulas?
A: _____

Lesson 32.

Q: What is improvisation?
A: _____

Q: What is needed to develop this skill?
A: _____

Lesson 33.

Q: All great great guitar players have developed the ability to do what?
A: _____

Q: What additional skills does this help develop?
A: _____

Lesson 34.

Q: What is ear training?
A: _____

Q: What else do you develop by knowing this skill?
A: _____

Lesson 35.

Q: What keys are presented in this lesson?
A: _____

Q: What is their purpose?
A: _____

Thank you for taking this test. It is for your benefit that it is presented. If there are some answers you don't know, that's ok. No worries. There is a lot of information here and it takes time to learn. Just be patient with yourself and take it one step at a time.

Go back to lessons that need more study. Go back to exercises that need more practice and take notes in the additional pages to work out magical musical formulas.

All this with a steady practice routine on a daily basis is what's needed to become a lead guitar wizard. This book only presents the fundamentals as volume 2 is on its way.

By time you get this volume fully studied, practiced and understood, you'll be ready for the next level.

Once again best of luck to you in your studies and if you need any help feel free to contact me online at my website www.dwaynesguitarlessons.com and connect with me on social media.

Sincerely,
Dwayne Jenkins

www.ingramcontent.com/pod-product-compliance
Lightning Source LLC
Chambersburg PA
CBHW051421070526
44584CB00023B/3524